W9-BCT-399

CAMPING

BY SARA GREEN

BELLWETHER MEDIA • MINNEAPOLIS, MN

Jump into the cockpit and take flight with Pilot books. Your journey will take you on high-energy adventures as you learn about all that is wild, weird, fascinating, and fun!

This edition first published in 2013 by Bellwether Media, Inc.

No part of this publication may be reproduced in whole or in part without written permission of the publisher.
For information regarding permission, write to Bellwether Media, Inc., Attention: Permissions Department,
5357 Penn Avenue South, Minneapolis, MN 55419.

Library of Congress Cataloging-in-Publication Data

Green, Sara, 1964-
 Camping / by Sara Green.
   p. cm. – (Pilot books: outdoor adventures)
 Includes bibliographical references and index.
 Summary: "Engaging images accompany information about camping. The combination of high-interest subject matter
and narrative text is intended for students in grades 3 through 7"–Provided by publisher.
 ISBN 978-1-60014-794-4 (hardcover : alk. paper)
 1. Camping–Juvenile literature. I. Title.
 GV192.2.G74 2012
 796.54–dc23
                            2012014515

TABLE OF CONTENTS

THE GREAT OUTDOORS

A group of friends sits around a campfire roasting marshmallows and telling stories. The night sky above them is filled with millions of stars. Several tents are nearby. Inside the tents, sleeping bags are rolled out on top of **sleeping pads**. The campers will be warm and cozy during the night.

In the morning, the campers wake to the sounds of birds chirping. They smell pancakes and bacon cooking on the stove. One camper rose early to prepare breakfast. Soon, everyone is out of the tents and sitting around the **fire ring**. It's time to eat!

Into the Wild

In the United States, around 40 million people go camping every year.

Camping is a **recreational** activity in which people spend one or more nights outdoors. Some campers sleep in tents or on the ground under the stars. Others prefer the comfort of a **recreational vehicle**, or RV. People can camp in their own backyards or travel far from home. Camping in national, state, and county parks is popular. Many forests and recreation areas also offer campsites.

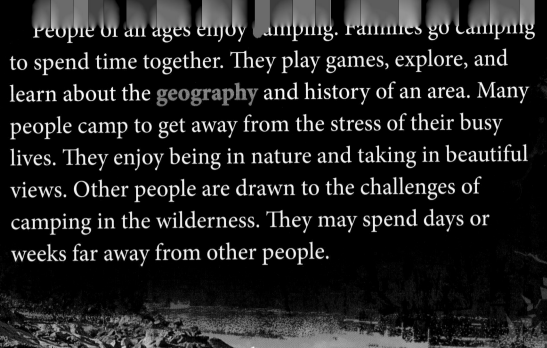

People of all ages enjoy camping. Families go camping to spend time together. They play games, explore, and learn about the **geography** and history of an area. Many people camp to get away from the stress of their busy lives. They enjoy being in nature and taking in beautiful views. Other people are drawn to the challenges of camping in the wilderness. They may spend days or weeks far away from other people.

recreational vehicle

Most people camp in the spring, summer, or fall. Before a trip, campers should learn about their destination's weather and landscape. They should be able to identify some of the area's plants and animals, especially poisonous ones. National parks and other popular locations get very crowded during the warm seasons. Their campgrounds fill up quickly, so people often need to make reservations to get a campsite.

Some adventurous people enjoy camping in cold areas during the winter months. They appreciate the beauty and quiet of the season. They do not have to deal with bug bites or large crowds. Winter campers stay comfortable by using tents and equipment made for cold weather. They often have to snowshoe or ski to their campsite.

People have many options for how to camp. Some campers want to create a home away from home. They travel to campgrounds by car and park near their tents. This is called **car camping**. Car campers often bring a lot to the campground. Common items include chairs, games, coolers, and bicycles. Many campgrounds have campsites for RVs. They have extra room for parking and provide **hookups** for electricity and water.

Some campgrounds have indoor bathrooms and running water. Others are **primitive**. Campers must bring their own water and use **pit toilets**. More adventurous people prefer to camp in the **backcountry**. A **permit** is required for most backcountry camping. This kind of camping is very rugged. Campers carry all of their gear on their backs. When they stop for the day, they must search for a suitable place to set up a tent and build a fire.

CAMPING EQUIPMENT

All types of camping require basic equipment. Most campers bring a tent, **rain fly**, sleeping bag, and sleeping pad. Tents are made of a strong, lightweight fabric called nylon. The **water-repellent** rain fly protects the tent in case of rain.

Any Size, Any Shape

The smallest tents have space for only one person. Larger tents can have multiple rooms and space for more than 10 people!

rain fly

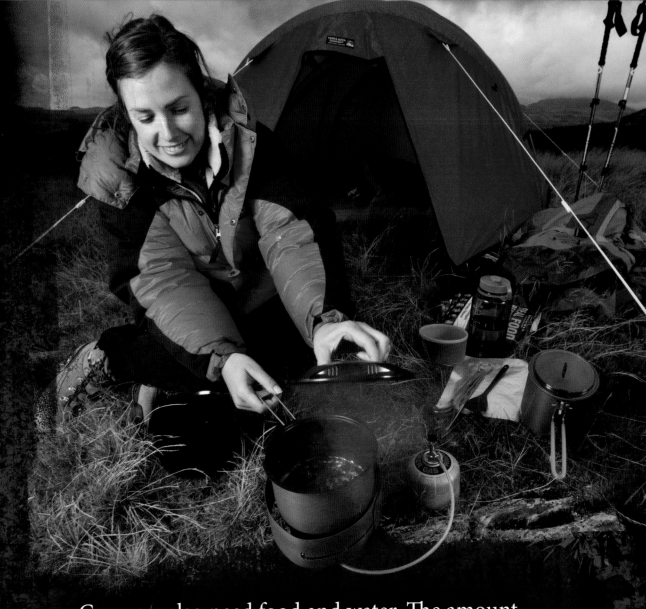

Campers also need food and water. The amount depends on the type and length of the trip. Car campers have more space. They often bring their food and drinks in coolers. They may even pack portable camping stoves. Backcountry campers travel light and carry food that won't spoil. Oatmeal, dry noodles, and rice are easy to prepare over a fire or lightweight stove.

Backcountry camping requires more planning than car camping. Backpackers must be prepared for all types of weather and emergencies. The backcountry does not always have marked trails. Backpackers must know how to read a **topographic map** and use a compass to avoid getting lost.

Most backpackers wear sturdy hiking boots and layered clothing to stay comfortable. They also carry waterproof jackets in case of rain.

Backpackers often rely on water from natural sources. They carry **water purifiers** to make the water safe to drink. Rope is also useful. When backpackers arrive at a campsite, they use the rope to tie bags of food high in a tree. This prevents bears, raccoons, and other animals from getting into the food.

Camping Checklist: The Basics

- Tent with rain fly
- Sleeping bag
- Sleeping pad
- Rain gear
- Warm clothes
- Flashlight / Lantern
- Food and water
- Cooking and eating tools
- Matches and other fire starters
- Sturdy walking shoes or hiking boots

RESPECT AND THE ENVIRONMENT

Whether camping in a busy campground or in the wilderness, campers should be respectful of other campers and nature. Most campgrounds have rules posted at the entrance. These often include rules about campfires, pets, and noise levels. If campsites are close together, it is important to be quiet at night and to keep lights off or low. People should also keep their campsites clean to prevent trash from blowing into neighboring sites.

Camping is a great way to experience wildlife. Some people are tempted to feed or touch animals, but it is best to just watch them from a distance. This keeps both campers and wildlife safe. Campers should always cook far from their tents and keep food out of the tents. This helps keep sleeping areas free of curious animals.

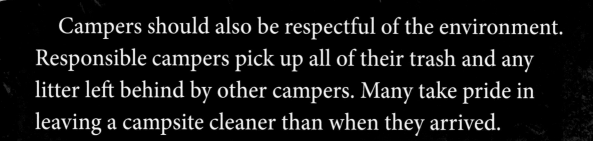

Campers should also be respectful of the environment. Responsible campers pick up all of their trash and any litter left behind by other campers. Many take pride in leaving a campsite cleaner than when they arrived.

People should never cut down trees for firewood. They should only use as much firewood as they need. Campers need to make sure their fire is completely out before they leave. Taking care of the land around campsites ensures that others will be able to have fun camping experiences.

Campfire Safety Tips

- If there is no fire ring, dig a small pit far away from shrubs, trees, and low-hanging branches

- Surround the pit with rocks and clear the ground around it

- Keep a bucket of water nearby

- Keep extra firewood a safe distance from the fire

- Never leave the fire unattended

- Extinguish the campfire completely before leaving

CAMPING
MOUNT RAINIER NATIONAL PARK

Millions of people camp in the 58 national parks of the United States each year. One of the most visited parks is Mount Rainier National Park near Seattle, Washington. Mount Rainier is an active volcano that rises 14,410 feet (4,392 meters) above sea level. The park is known for its **glaciers**, waterfalls, forests, and meadows. It offers more than 500 campsites. Many require reservations, especially in the summer.

During their stay, campers can mountain bike, hike, ride horses, and fish. **Park rangers** lead hikes on mountain trails and evening talks under the stars. One of the park's most popular camping spots is the Mowich Lake Campground. Campers enjoy a magnificent view of Mount Rainier from the shore of a

GLOSSARY

backcountry—wilderness; backcountry has little to no human development.

car camping—camping at a site that has a spot to park a car

fire ring—a metal or stone ring used to contain campfires

geography—the study of the physical features of the earth

glaciers—massive sheets of ice that cover a large area of land

hookups—places where recreational vehicles can connect to electricity and water

park rangers—people who protect and preserve parks; park rangers also enforce park rules.

permit—a document that gives legal permission to do an activity

pit toilets—holes in the ground that are used as toilets

primitive—without conveniences such as running water and electricity

rain fly—a piece of canvas that covers a tent to protect it from getting wet

recreational—done for enjoyment

recreational vehicle—a large vehicle that people often stay in while camping

sleeping pads—cushioned pads that provide comfort and protect campers from the cold ground

spoil—to go bad

topographic map—a type of map that shows both the natural and artificial features of a landscape

water purifiers—filters or tablets that remove unhealthy materials from water to make it safe to drink

water-repellent—made of material that does not soak up water

TO LEARN MORE

At the Library

Brunelle, Lynn. *Camp Out! The Ultimate Kids' Guide, from the Backyard to the Backwoods.* New York, N.Y.: Workman Pub., 2007.

George, Kristine O'Connell. *Toasting Marshmallows: Camping Poems.* New York, N.Y.: Clarion Books, 2001.

Ruurs, Margriet. *When We Go Camping.* Toronto, Ont.: Tundra, 2001.

On the Web

Learning more about camping is as easy as 1, 2, 3.

1. Go to www.factsurfer.com.

2. Enter "camping" into the search box.

3. Click the "Surf" button and you will see a list of related Web sites.

With factsurfer.com, finding more information is just a click away.

INDEX